ENTREPRENEUR SUCCESSFUL

ENTREPRENEUR
SUCCESSFUL

 ENTREPRENEUR SUCCESSFUL

 ENTREPRENEUR SUCCESSFUL

INDEX

We begin...

Today isn't everything, really.

Set the goal now, for tomorrow's benefit

Growing and Staying Green

How to understand your market

Trends vs. Trend Setter

Home: History

Investing in knowledge

Growth success without potential waste

Management of monetary principles

Marketing for true success

Principles to remember and use

Final thoughts

ENTREPRENEUR SUCCESSFUL

We begin...

What does it mean to you to be an entrepreneur?

Anyone who is interested in finding true success throughout their lives can do so, with the right tools, the right amount of ambition and the knowledge to make it all happen. However, the entrepreneur, no matter what business he or she is in, must plan ahead and find success through much more than these things.

To be an entrepreneur, you're not just looking for benefits right now. While you're sure you want your business to really take off and do well in your first year, your childhood is just as important, if not more so, that the long-term goals you have match the need you have as well.

In the long run, the entrepreneurial world is very different and much more unique. To find true success, you need to think about both the present and the future, twice as much.

How and what will you do to make sure that your business, the one you've worked so hard to make happen in the first place, does it in the long run? While this is not an easy thing to do, you can do it skillfully.

In this e-book, you will learn some of the most essential principles to protect your

business not only today, but also in the long run.

As a new entrepreneur or aspiring entrepreneur, you didn't think about what the future would hold for you because only the present mattered. Now, however, is the perfect time to step back and discover the best way to run your business in the long run.

If you want to have a business that will allow you to be successful and have money in your pocket in the future, it is essential that you spend some time planning for this to happen.

The good news is that you don't have to go to school or be a space scientist to realize this. In fact, we provide a great deal of information and resources that you need here, without having to look anywhere else.

Of course, we also hope that you will feel inspired to take the next step and find the real benefit of your business by putting these things into action in the first place. When you do these things, real success and the money in your wallet is all that matters.

 ENTREPRENEUR SUCCESSFUL

Today isn't everything, really.

As an entrepreneur, your work is very detailed. You have to be the creative one. You have to be the boss. You need to keep your business vision at the forefront of every single thing you do for that business. But, today is not all.

As a business owner, you must remember the fact that the long-term goals and process of your business can only happen if you plan for it now, not in the day.

You've probably heard people say you need

to do it; "Live the day!" As an entrepreneur, this is not possible and should not be the way you maintain your business agenda.

But why not?

Most of the time, we'd like to think that all we really need to do is make a plan and hold on to it. Somehow, things will be put in place. You have to. It's all you can do.

However, from a business point of view, there is a lot more to think about.

For example, you may have employees who need funds from your business for their daily expenses.

 ENTREPRENEUR SUCCESSFUL

You may need to consider the overall benefits you have to keep your business going. What about your assets? Will they survive the process? What about your cash flow? What if something goes wrong?

All of these things are really just the tip of the iceberg when it comes to ruining a long-term business. The bottom line is that you need to consider what your business will be like today, as well as ten, twenty and more years later.

Think about this

Before you begin, it is essential that you understand two concepts of your business. When making a business decision, ask yourself these questions first.

1- When I make this decision, what are the immediate and short-term effects of doing so? How does this affect my business today?

2. When I make this decision, what is the long-term effect of making this decision? How will this decision affect my business in a few months and years?

When you take the time to carefully consider the decisions that occur in front of you, you put yourself in charge of your destiny.

If you allow the cards to fall where they can, you may not be in business within six months. So, as you work with this e-book, ask yourself what steps you can take right

now that will improve your overall business in the short and long term.

Of course, we must mention that there is never a sure way to know what the future holds. There is no way to know if you are really making the right decision or not. But, what you have to do here is make sure you give tomorrow the best possible opportunity.

Don't let it happen, make today count for tomorrow and tomorrow for tomorrow.

Set the goal now, for tomorrow's benefit

No matter what aspect of your life you are talking about, goal setting is a crucial factor throughout the process. As you will see, every decision you make as an entrepreneur will affect your overall goal of succeeding with your business. However, it is much more than that.

You should also set goals because they can help you make the right decisions throughout the process of reaching the level of success that lies ahead. By investing the time and energy you have to set goals now, you help yourself in every decision you make

to achieve the end result you expect.

In other words, if you set some overall goals today, you can help ensure that your business will be there and will be prosperous throughout the future of the business. Goals now count.

While we all have the same goal of achieving success in the future, we have yet to set goals that will help us reach that point. It doesn't happen overnight!

How to set goals successfully

When it comes to setting goals, there aren't many of us who are very good at it. There are many opportunities to make mistakes,

but the real problem is how we make them and what we do once we make them.

To begin with, it's essential to know what your goals are. Take a few minutes right now to resolve this. Just sit down with a blank sheet of paper (yes, you can use your computer too!) and avoid all distractions for ten minutes.

Write down anything that comes to mind regarding your goals.

What are they?

Where do you want to be in a year?

ENTREPRENEUR SUCCESSFUL

Who do you want to have with you?

Where do you see your business in five years? 20?

How much dollar sales will make you happy this year?

What do you need to earn in profits to reach a new level of satisfaction each year?

All of these things can be things that awaken your mind. Determine where your business will be in the next few years. For starters, look long term. Then follow these tips.

ENTREPRENEUR SUCCESSFUL

Writing goals is made easy through a few basic steps.

1. Write down your long-term goal. This is where you want to be in several years, or where you need to be to be as successful as you plan to be.

2. Give yourself a time frame to make that happen. You may want to say that you want to make your first million in two years. Or, it may take many more for that to happen. Giving your goal a time frame helps your mind set on how to make that happen. If you leave it open, long-term goals are not benefited by your actions every day, as they would be here.

3. Give yourself smaller goals to achieve as

you move toward the larger one. For example, the new entrepreneur may say that he wants to be in an office, established and functioning within a month. In six months, he plans to make a profit after expenses have been paid. Determine what your steps are to reach your goal. Be sure to write them down with time frames attached as well.

4. Now, handwrite them on paper as follows. "Within six months, I will have paid off all my debt and be safe. I'll do it by pushing sales and not pushing any new expenses during that time. In this way, you have listed not only what the goal and time frame is to achieve it, but also how you will achieve it.

5. Take this piece of paper and place it everywhere and anywhere where you can see it at least several times a day. Seeing it will

allow you to think about it. Thinking about it makes it happen. Success through goals is the only way to find it.

Now that you know what your goals are, it is essential that you make sure they are met.

You will need to read those goals every day, at least once a day. When you think about it, you see it, you feel it, you make it happen.Over the next few chapters, we'll discuss the long-term decisions you need to make, as well as the various things you need to do to get them done.

When you go through each step, determine your goal for it. How will you implement it in your current workday and how will you make sure it happens?

Growing and Staying Green

When you're green, you're growing. Once you start turning red, you're expiring. Don't you want to be always green then?

As an entrepreneur, one thing to keep in mind is that the world never stays the same. For the most part, you are always going to find some changes happening. As a business owner, if you can't adjust your business to those changes, you may encounter more problems than benefits.

Many businesses have had to close simply

because their product no longer works with what the consumer needs. Nor does it matter what kind of business you have. The bottom line is that if you're not green and you're growing, you're not going to be in business for long.

Is your business green and growing?

The Long-Term Goal

The long-term objective of any business situation is to ensure that they are able to meet the needs of the customer or consumer. If they cannot do this, they cannot have consumers and will eventually fall outside the scope of application. If they do, they will continually find rewards with higher profits and new customers to fill their pockets.

In this case, the long-term goal you need to make is to keep the green. You need to maintain some aspect that will continually help you move forward with what is happening within your business.

If you are not sure why it is important, for example, the current situation.

Today, we hear a lot about the cost of energy, the cost of gas and all that goes with it. In fact, today, more people than ever know what a barrel of crude oil costs. Why is this; and what does this do for the industry?

If you haven't spent time buying or buying a car, you may not realize that many manufacturers are struggling to stay in business. Your problem is that your cars, trucks or anything in between are not able to meet the demands of the consumer.

Why not? They may not be able to offer low enough mileage. With each passing year, more and more consumers are looking for a better way to meet their energy needs. This stands in the way of cars that are hybrids and those that do not run on petrol.

In these cases, if the company cannot meet the needs of the consumer, how can they run efficient businesses?

They can't, and that's the same thing that can happen to virtually any business. Unless your business can be green, growing and

exploring new routes to take, it cannot meet the needs of the consumer, which is, of course, the soul of the business.

How to

The question you must ask yourself, then, is what do you need to do to make this happen in your business?

Let's say you have an Internet business. Maybe one of the important things you should do is keep up with search engine optimization.

If you don't follow and keep in touch with the new rules and the changing scheme of issues, your website will not be well positioned and you will go outside the scope of what is worthwhile.

In this case, it is essential that you maintain the ability to maintain your knowledge and skills in the highest quality. The same is true of other businesses, such as insurance agencies and real estate agencies. Unless you keep your knowledge at the top, you can't be sure you're doing the right thing.

There are other ways you need to think about this as well. For example, what about marketing? If your marketing is not modern enough (or turns out to be too modern for the wrong market), you may be in trouble.

In this case, it's essential that you find a way to reach the right audience with the right medium and keep it up to date. You already know how to market your business; just make sure you stay current on how to do it as the market changes.

What other aspects of your business might you think have the same potential for your attention?

Finding the various ways to stay fresh can include keeping your business product fresh, with the latest technology and features that suit the consumer's needs and even reinventing yourself to make sure the business always stays on top.

When you invest time and money in staying green, the business always has the potential for success.

Understanding the ever-changing consumer

One of the most difficult things you will have to do as an entrepreneur is to make sure that you meet the needs of your consumers. The hard part of all this is not the fact that you need to do it, but rather the way you understand consumers.

Some companies spend millions of dollars on research each year to ensure that their product or sales pitch is welcomed by the economy. The scary factors are that, even with all that, they continue to risk a lot and often fail at what they are doing.

This can make the small business owner wonder how he can afford to make this happen.

Understanding the consumer is not an easy task. However, it is essential that someone works hard to find this information.

If you are interested, you can do so by hiring a company to conduct your market research. This can be a solid decision that is provided at a decent cost to you. Depending on your specific business and product, as well as your marketing budget, this may be a good choice for you.

On the other hand, it may not be something you want to pursue. In that case, it is essential that you invest some time in finding the right solution through other means. No matter what you do, from talking to your customers individually to observing market trends in what your competitors do, the goal is to ensure that you continue to offer the best possible product.

To make sure you are green; compare what you have to offer to the other consumer options. What do you have that makes them a better choice about you?

When you can answer that and then address it, you will be green and grow, growing toward profits, of course.

How to understand your market

One thing we need to mention is that the market you face is likely to be very different from the market someone else is facing. The goals you have compared to someone else's goals are very different. In fact, you are sure that you will see yourself striving for profits that are not commensurate with your business objectives.

First, take a step back, out of the picture and look at your market.

If you are selling on the Internet, look at the

other sellers.

If you own a small local business, step back and look at your local market.

Whatever you're doing, go back.

To consider now

The market you work in depends to a large extent on who your customers are. If you're looking for immediate success, simply opening your doors can help you get started. But, by looking at your market, you can see several things better.

Ask yourself and answer these questions

before you move on.

- Who is my customer? Older people or children, business women or the business owner... determine who your customer is.

- How do they find you? Do they find you online, through a simple web search? Do they need to find you through an affiliate link? Do they find you in their local area, in one of the most popular areas of the city?

- Who else is out there? Who is your competition? Where are they? What do they offer that allows you to improve them? How do they improve you in your market? Why are they open, driving business away from you?

- What do you offer that is somehow better than the other guy? What do they offer that is somehow better than you?

- Where is your market going? Is the economy growing, stagnating or stable? How much money do your customers have to spend on your product?

You can go on and on with the things you should be considering about your own specific business. Understanding your market is crucial to understanding what your future is.

If you don't know who your consumer is, how do you know how it's changing?

In addition, you need to know what to expect from the market around you. If you realize that the economy is falling, you may need to go back and look to the future in a different way. If you look at your market and see that your competition has taken your product in a different way and is succeeding with that, you need to make a move. How do you compete? What will you offer that will be better? Also, how will you take the next step toward success? How will you improve them?

Paying attention

By paying attention to your market, you will make better decisions. When you look toward the long-term goals you have in place to keep your business going, you need to make sure that your market is one of the top priorities you have.

If you don't invest time in staying in that market, or even expanding out of it, you can't and won't make things work. Business cannot grow or stay green without constant vigilance of the market around it.

In later chapters we will talk more about growth and how to visualize its future in this regard. However, it is important to keep in mind that you have to be on the lookout for signs that the market needs more of your product or is not detecting it.

There is no doubt that some of these things are essential to do, but some can be difficult to do as well. However, if you don't invest the time needed to analyze and understand the customer you have, how will you make it work?

Again, you have the ability to hire someone to do this job for you. But, you can and should consider not only doing this, but also helping yourself with your own research and knowledge.

Being a physical presence in your market (even on the web) helps you make sure that people can come to you. It allows you to see your market firsthand and therefore make good decisions.

Trends vs. Trend Setter

Is your business a trendsetter? Or is it following the trend?

If you're not sure, consider how this plays a role in your future.

As a trend setter, you are always one step ahead of the game. What you do, others admire, but not just this once. If you can accomplish this often by setting the trend that is, you can even create the fact that you will have others looking to you to set the next trend.

On the other hand, if you are following the trend, things are not so good. You will have to make up time for the other product or business that is going well for you. You have lost precious sales time in the process. In addition, you will always have to watch the other guy to see what is going to happen next, rather than being in charge of what is. This can be a challenging place to be, actually.

Take a minute to think about where you are in this equation.

Do you tend to follow someone else's lead, hoping there's enough in the pot for you too? Or, are you looking for something new and exciting and trying to incorporate it into your business?

Depending on your current position, this will help you see how it affects your long-term goals and your ability to achieve the success you want.

Long-term trend?

We all know that trends come and go. You should also realize that not all of them are the right path for every business. However, trend is something to pay attention to when it comes to your long-term success.

As we mentioned, the benefits of setting the trend in your market are not based solely on the basics of selling. Sure, if you can get a monopoly on a product for a few days, weeks

or more, you're going to have some impressive sales to take advantage of.

However, those sales soon disappear. In the short term, that's all that matters. But, in this case, we're talking about long-term goals.

If you are the trendsetter, then your long-term benefits of being in this business is that you have more ability and movement to establish the next trend as well.

Some companies in the market do not have the ability to perfectly meet the needs of their customers. Some will only succeed from time to time when it comes to trends. However, the company that is able to establish some trends can ensure a greater ability in the future to do the same.

When a company has other companies looking for the next trend, guess who is going to be successful in the long run?

Consider Your Reputation

This is the only factor that plays a role in the development of your reputation as a company as well. Not all companies can say they have a good reputation with their consumers in the long run. However, those who do can almost count on a monopoly in their market.

Take, for example, Mom and Dad's stores, which are so often on the outskirts of their prime. Why are they such good places to go?

It's because they have a solid reputation for providing success and doing well with their product. Even if your product is old-fashioned, it is still something you want and need because of its quality. That helps finance true success with the market.

Of course, your reputation comes into play for more reasons or ways than just this. The fact is that it also happens when you consider customer service, prices, good community connections and so on. All of these things play a role in your reputation, just to name a few!

When you are considering your long-term goal of success and having good money in your pocket, how does your reputation play a role?

We talk about how this happens with trend setting, but it can go further. In today's offline world, it's hard to get a good cup of coffee without begging. It doesn't matter if you are online or offline with your product, however, you can earn many rewards and profits by just providing good service.

Building a reputation is essential for continued growth. However, remember that a reputation can go both ways (good and bad!) So make sure you have a solid backing of satisfied customers in your market. This will be worth it for you today, as well as for the future.

Home: History

One thing many business owners don't take enough into account is their history and the learning they have learned from it. When you consider how your story affects your future potential, you can see better why it's essential that this is something you pay a good deal of attention to.

Do you learn from history?

Many of us will remember the times our parents scolded us. "Don't ever do that again!" "Learn from your mistakes." All of these things are very important in the business world as well.

In this principle that is crucial to the success of your business, you need to take into consideration your past and where you have been to help you figure out where you and your business are headed.

Questions to consider

Now, to begin with this director, consider these questions.

1- Where have you been and what have you learned? When you think of the past, determine what it means to find success in this way. What background do you have that has taught you something that could play a role in your life and well-being today?

2- What have you learned from mistakes? Every entrepreneur makes mistakes while working in his or her business. Whether you're new or an experienced professional, mistakes can happen once for many reasons. But the difference is that if you allow it to happen again. If not, then you may find success much easier and faster than if you repeat the same mistake over and over again.

3- What would you have liked to do differently? Regrets don't have to be wasted this time. As an entrepreneur, you may have several regrets in mind. Perhaps you feel as if you have wasted a great deal of time getting your business up and running. Now, take this regret and determine what you would do today. Would you start your business before? Put more into it before?

Understanding these aspects of your past can help you in the long run. Of course, we don't want to keep making the same mistakes, but there aren't many entrepreneurs who do.

Instead, most of us will learn from our mistakes, but only if we take the time to look at them and see what they were and how they could be avoided.

Your story is yours alone. Whether it's a story about your personal life and business or just about the company, it's essential that you stop and look and learn.

Making mistakes today is not easy. No one wants to do it, but if it happens to you, do the following.

1. Recognize that something didn't go right. Don't get angry about it (if possible) and realize that something went wrong.

2. Determine what it was and how it happened. Getting the whole story, learning the whole puzzle will allow a better understanding. Learning how it happened allows you to see in detail what the mistake was.

3. Decide to improve your chances of not letting that mistake happen again. To do this, be sure to spend the necessary time making decisions to avoid this problem.

Not all stories are bad

It is important to note that history does not always have to tell you the wrong side of things. You can and should see the good things that have happened in your story as well. What led you to this level of success in which you find yourself today? What makes that first sale happen and happen so well?

Taking a look at the good things that have happened in the past is part of the principle of looking to the past for answers for your future. They allow you to see a real benefit for the good that has happened in your business. You may even be able to take note of how the good has happened so that it happens again and again in the future of your business as well.

When you take the time to analyze all the good and bad that has happened in your past, you can make sure that profits come in the future, while mistakes don't. You can also take the time to analyze all the good and bad that has happened in your past, you can make sure that profits come in the future, while mistakes don't.

As part of your future success, you must understand your history and how to secure the future through this enormous amount of knowledge that you have. Believe it or not, this is a personal touch and an experience that no one else can have.

Investing in knowledge

If you are like many entrepreneurs, then you know that it is essential to have good knowledge when it comes to running your business.

As we've discussed, it's important to make sure that those who provide you with the necessary information do so without taking all your money just so that you can spend more.

For example, some of the most common mistakes that entrepreneurs who are just starting out make is that they just keep buying information. This is especially true in

the case of those who are starting an online business.

There is no doubt that you need to have a good amount of knowledge to make something happen. You need to know how to get started, you need to know what steps to take and you need to know where to do all this. But, there is a limit.

One thing to keep in mind is your ability to make decisions. Once you have purchased the latest version of the kit, keep in mind that you are ready to make some decisions.

If you buy a kit or program and see another one that seems to offer some additional benefits, you may be tempted to buy that one as well. After all, it can't hurt to have more information, can it?

It doesn't hurt to have a good amount of information, except the wallet, of course. However, that's not the problem. The problem is what you do with it.

A Beginning

There are a number of things you can do to make this happen to you. Remember this principle.

If you find yourself buying one product after another, you are not thinking about your next productive move, but rather about standing firm.

If you buy a product to benefit your business, it is essential that you use it and make the most of it before moving on to the next purchase.

Making it worth your while

In later chapters we will talk about the fact that you need to manage your money closely, but for now, you must realize that the investment in any asset or tool that benefits your business must be used in its entirety to make it a smart investment.

No matter what business you're in, if you don't take the time to invest in a business product wisely, you're literally throwing away your profits.

If you fall victim to all those stratagems to buy this greta kit or that sure method of making a million dollars, sure you are helping someone else make that million dollars.

That doesn't mean you shouldn't buy any of them. Instead, select the one that provides you with the best resources, invest in it wisely and then use it fully, incorporating everything that needs to be incorporated into the plan.

When you do this, your investment is beneficial to your business. If you simply move on to the following, you find yourself facing not benefits, but risks and an empty wallet that accompanies you

Making wise decisions

In our next chapters, we will touch on some very important assets, including their cash flow. But, before we do that, we need to touch the principle of making the right decisions regarding your business.

How are decisions made? Do you make impulsive choices of the moment because that's the way you feel that day?

Do you work hard to find the right solution, to the point that when you make the decision it's already too late?

If you do these things, you are not benefiting

your business, but rather letting the cards fall where they should. This is a big problem for the vast majority of start-up entrepreneurs. Making wise decisions is not easy, but it must be done, though.

Once you realize how you are making a decision, you can begin to correct it. To help you make the right decisions, follow these steps and tips to ensure the right decisions without letting them slip through your fingers.

Decision-Making Tips

Making a decision is hard work. Here are some tips to help you.

ENTREPRENEUR SUCCESSFUL

1. Invest time in learning about the possible product or problem you face. If you're trying to decide whether or not to buy a product, consider what you'll do to improve the performance of your business. What can you do for yourself?

2. Spend some time researching possible solutions, both what you have found and what you have not found. What can you do about your problem? What is the lowest cost you can find? What are the potential risks of this article?

3. After this, determine if the investment is worth it for your own well-being or that of your business. Waiting until after learning more about the product will allow you to make a decision at the conclusion of the research you have done.

4. If you can't decide within a few days, then maybe you don't know about this topic or choice to determine what is suitable for your business. Let it go and forget it. Or, look for another option. Don't stop there.

Making the right decisions also means that you need to realize your current state of affairs.

If your business isn't attracting profits because you don't have the necessary tools, it's time to invest in new tools; otherwise your business won't be there long enough for you to worry about it.

If your business is doing well and you don't

have to hang up, then don't invest in something that doesn't have a direct return on your profit margin.

Most entrepreneurs have tons of people coming to them offering them a wide range of different benefits, products and services because, like you, they are looking to make their business work. Don't fall into the trap of these businessmen who think they can solve your problems. While it may seem difficult to make good decisions regarding the business you have, it is imperative that you learn to trust yourself. If you don't trust your decisions, you can't run a business.

This is also a principle you need to realize: If you don't trust yourself, you can't ruin a successful business.

Growth success without potential waste

One of the long-term things every entrepreneur should think about is growth.

Growth is the expansion of your business to the next level. This could mean expanding your business to include more products, doing more things, or growing physically by adding more locations.

Growth is what has the potential for greater long-term success. An entrepreneur can find many benefits for himself if he manages to grow carefully, without going too far or stretching too fast.

If that sounds hard to do, it can be. Many companies have failed to expand too quickly and not have enough market share to keep them together. On the other hand, there are many companies that have not grown as much as they could and are now missing out on the largest potential profit margin.

It is also personal

Of course, growing your business is a personal choice. Not everyone can determine where you are here at the beginning of your business as well. However, one thing is for sure.

Your growth potential has a lot to do with the security of your business. If you have confidence and assurance that your business is a business worth existing, then by all means you can grow. If you're not sure and can't make decisions regarding the growth of your business, you can't grow.

While most people are ready and willing to take full advantage of the opportunity to build on what they have created, others are willing to let things fall as they can.

One principle you need to remember, then, is that in order to be successful in your business, you need to determine your level of security at risk. With what do you feel comfortable with and how can you be sure that what you are doing is what will be worthwhile in the long run?

These are hard questions to answer, but they must be asked.

Growing up too fast

One of the worst things you can do for your business is grow too fast. If you don't have the assets and cash flow to support this type of major expansion, you may face a series of problems just to keep your business rather than worry about expanding it.

The risk of failure due to over-expansion too quickly is that you may not be able to handle the obligations of multiple locations or such a large corporation. Many of the large corporations that have faced this have failed

because of the enormous expense of assuming another building, another payroll, another unit.

However, the owner of the smallest business does not face this huge number of risks as the largest corporation. But!

It is important to ensure that you invest wisely in growth and not without first investing time. Determining where your potential profits are is the first key to success. In addition, a good look at what the possibilities are is in order.

Are you ready to grow?

Those who are interested in finding the right

solution in terms of growth are doing the right thing. However, remember that it is important to make a decision in the right mood and with the right amount of research done in the first place.

In terms of growth, what the right choice is is up to you individually. Ask these questions about your success:

Does your business have the cash flow to support not only this location in operation (or your current business) as well as another?

If you are expanding, what makes you believe that this expansion will serve your business well?

What is the likely expense of growth and does the business have the means to protect and cover that cost?

All of these things are crucial to the success of your business in the growth factor. But, you also need to make sure that you don't limit your growth with insufficient opportunities.

Don't limit it

The mistake of many business owners is that they don't put their foot out there and expand fast enough or don't do it at all. While it is essential not to move too fast, it is equally important to consider whether you are moving too slowly to benefit.

To understand this factor, you need to get back to your business. Are you getting everything you can out of it? Can you do more or get a better end result if you grow in some way?

To learn the right amount of growth for your business, you can do test market studies, invest in surveys, or just start slowly and work your way up to it. The amount you invest in your business depends on you and how well the company has done so far.

A bad business that is not working well in one place may not work well in another.

A good business that is thriving can be hampered by not moving it.

Of course, the opposite is also true. Research is the best way to determine where your business is growing.

Management of monetary principles

What makes you profitable as a business owner? In the next chapter, we'll look at ways you should manage your cash flow and assets if you plan to have money in your pocket for the long term.

Do you have the ability to think, analyze and ultimately decide on business related decisions?

As we've discussed, your ability to do these things is what will stop them or push them forward both today and in the future. Now, take those ideas and determine how well they fit into your ability to make decisions about the success of your business where the profit margin is important.

Throughout this chapter we will discuss several aspects in detail, allowing you to fully understand what you need to do to be successful in terms of the profitability of your business.

Controlling Your Money, Right

Do you have what it takes to manage your money? If not, it's time to find someone who can do it for you. Without strict control over the finances of your business, there is no way to know what the future may or may not hold. That doesn't mean you can't spend

money. This is a big mistake that people make.

Instead, as an entrepreneur and business owner, you need to learn to spend money the right way.

The first thing you need to do is determine a budget for the success of your business. This should be a global budget in the beginning. Things to consider include:

- Manage expenses to keep the business running smoothly.

- Manage your business debt due to growth or start-up costs (to pay them off successfully).

- Managing profits, if available, should be done with an idea of how much is going to be invested in the business and what is going to go to other beneficial needs that the business has.

The budget must be done carefully, with a good dose of reflection on each of these areas. Instead of a dollar montage, the business budget should be done by percentages.

Perhaps 20 percent of the profits will go toward investing in the business, while the rest of the profits will go toward paying off the debt. Any percentage you feel comfortable with should be taken into account here.

Beyond the budgetary aspect of fund management are the strictly organizational aspects that need to be taken into account. Good quality and detailed accounting is necessary to manage the overall success of the business and the funds down to the last detail.

In addition, measures need to be taken to manage unforeseen expenses and even ensure that everything is under control.

Although this seems obvious, many companies fail due to mismanagement of money in the initial stages. Don't get caught up in the "I don't have time now, I'll do it later" scam. Without doing this from the beginning, it won't happen in your entire business.

Don't you think you need it?

If you don't think you need to do this kind of detailed accounting for your business, you are preparing for a big failure. Now, this doesn't mean you can't make a profit by being careless, but remember, we're talking long-term.

Even very large international companies are very careful with the fate of every penny they spend. After all, this is money that could be doing something for the business, right? Whether you have hundreds of dollars to budget or billions of dollars, strict money management is the key to successfully financing any business through the good times and the bad.

Also, make sure you're also monitoring these numbers. It doesn't do you any good to get a system up and running and use it, but don't use it to its fullest. The fact is that you should be doing these things:

- Determine where the money is going and if it is being done accurately.

- Determine where you can reduce costs and expenses.

- Determine what you can do differently for less funds, without jeopardizing the real quality of your business.

Being a little tight with your business is not a bad thing, assuming you take care of all aspects of the business need, including reinvestment and growth potential as well.

You're Cash Flow

The next money management principle to consider is your cash flow principle. Without having a good amount of cash flow in your business, it will sink.

If you own a small business, it is even more important to do this simply because there is nothing and no one behind you to support that bad year or that great accident that has occurred. Loans are just as good and are not good at all if you can't get them.

The ability to maintain your cash flow is the key to a successful, long-term business. Without careful cash flow management, your business will not survive lean times or even the best.

How do you do this? There are several things to keep in mind here.

First, you must make sure that as an entrepreneur you have a good strong hand in the cash flow of your business. You should be able to monitor it personally every day.

Does this sound like too much? If you don't, you may not know what your business situation is on any given day. That can lead to potential long-term problems with your success.

Carefully consider each and every expense. As an entrepreneur, you need to make these decisions wisely. Just as growing too fast can hurt you; it can also hurt you not having the cash flow to support your business in the short or long term.

In addition, you should personally monitor your budget, your expenses, your earnings and your ability to use every dollar you have wisely. After all, that's what those budgets are for. Use them, keep them, and work every dollar to get the most out of it.

Two principles to remember

When it comes to business success, you'll

have to consider these two principles when it comes to how money management goes.

First, consider this: You should only spend money when there is a potential to earn money from that spending.

It's self-explanatory, isn't it? You shouldn't be making an investment in your business, especially a small business owner, unless it allows you to earn more money as a direct and end result.

Second, let's consider this: "If it's not an income, it's an expense."

How does that influence the business you're currently doing? Does it give you a chance to make a successful end of the month? Do you shop without thinking carefully about those dollars? If it's not an income for you, it's an expense.

Managing your cash flow successfully will allow your business to deposit funds instead of losing them. When you do this successfully, your business has the potential to be a long-term success. If you want to be there in the future, manage your money successfully, with an eye on almost every dollar you have.

It's not cheap, it's smart

Even if it seems like we tell you to be frugal or cheap with your business, you need to make sure that the funds you are spending are funds that are spent wisely, without wasting.

How can you be so frugal (that's a better name!) that you can find true success in doing so?

- Determine how you spend every dollar of your business budget.

- Is that dollar being spent in the best way possible? How is it being spent benefiting your bottom line?

- Is there a better way to spend that dollar? Can you get more for it with another company or service or another opportunity?

- Is there a better way to save your money, with better performance?

These are questions that any business owner should consider each and every day they own their business. What can you do better to save more in your business for your business?

Why do this?

How many millionaires, or even billionaires, have heard about still driving their old, ramshackle cars? Why do they do that when they can afford to have much prettier, more expensive cars?

ENTREPRENEUR SUCCESSFUL

It's not because they don't want to spend money or because they like to be cheap. The benefit here really comes from the fact that they like to save. Saving cash for your business is a great way to find real success because you will have those funds to use again and again when you need them.

Wal-Mart founder Sam Walton was worth $25 billion at one point in his career. Would you believe that even with that kind of value he still drove his old truck to work every day? Being frugal has its rewards because this is obviously what led him to a net worth of $25 billion.

When you are frugal, your business will prosper, year after year. If you're a spender, you won't have the funds to allow that to happen year after year, will you?

All these tips for saving money and handling cash may not seem like a big deal to you. If that's the case, they're already making them and finding success with them, or they're actually wasting money and not achieving the success they already want.

However, managing your funds wisely is one of the key components to your success in a small business. Every entrepreneur must take their time to do so or they will find themselves without the benefits they so desperately need.

In the end, is it worth being a little frugal to reach that huge multimillion-dollar net worth? There isn't a car in this world that can make that kind of promise to you, is there?

Be sure to install these benefits and money management principles into your daily routine and long-term goals within your business.

Marketing for true success

If you're an entrepreneur, marketing is something in your blood; it should at least be there if you plan to have customers.

But do you market your business for real success and long-term profits?

If you think so, you may not really understand the true potential of the right marketing tools.

What is marketing? Marketing is what attracts a customer to your business. You need to let others know that you are there and that you are ready and willing to provide them with a service.

However, that basic definition is not enough to take you through the entire marketing process for the success of your business.

If you want to be successful in the long run, take marketing much more seriously and follow these tips for various aspects of marketing.

Determine the potential of your products

Before you can be successful in marketing your business, you must take a good amount of time to determine what it is about what you that have others do want.

In other words, what does your product provide? A successful business will provide some sort of immediate satisfaction for a need someone has. You should consider this even before entering the business. What is it that your product has the potential to solve or fill the need?

In addition, you must determine how you can offer these things to your customers to improve their lives. Perhaps you can offer them something that solves a problem they have, but that is still something that is affordable to remedy that solution.

Having a clearly defined market benefit is essential to getting the most out of your product. People want to know, "What will

you do for me?" and "Why should I buy this for something else?"

When you can find out how this plays a role in your product's capabilities, you can see the right course of marketing that product. Answering these questions is what you must do to find the success defined here.

Pricing is also important

The next objective to be taken into account is that of price fixing. When it comes to marketing, you may not think about the price you put on your product, but this also matters. People move through sales and deals. They like a product that can provide them with the ability to solve their needs, but in a cost effective manner.

Without the right price, there is no difference in the way they market the product at the end.

What do people look for when it comes to the price of a product or service? They want something that is fair, not something that makes them go bankrupt. In addition, most people understand perfectly that there is a need for the company to make a profit. The problem comes when they are being taken advantage of.

In addition, competition is important in this case as well. If your product is better than another, maybe it should be more, but it shouldn't be scandalous because, if it is, no one will bother with it.

ENTREPRENEUR SUCCESSFUL

Consider its ability to be called a Unique Selling Proposition. This means that it will have similar, but at least unique, features that will allow it to compete with other products.

Of course, as we mentioned, your product must meet someone's need out there. But, if there are five different products doing that, it may be difficult for you to find your niche. Therefore, you must create for yourself a unique quality that will drive your marketing and your prices.

What makes your product better, in other words?

If you are a new business owner, for example, and are looking for a new product to invest in, you may not want to try to create your own product, service, or other component. Rather, you may decide that taking something that is already on the market and finding a way to do it even better, or at a better price, is the right way to do it.

Effective Marketing

Throughout this chapter we've talked about ways you can successfully market your business. Now, consider your sales profits.

Can you say that when each and every one of your employees (or just you) walks through the door, your goal is to satisfy a customer?

Not only to serve a customer, but also to satisfy him. If you can't say that, then perhaps your marketing in terms of sales is not working as effectively as it should.

This is what we mean. If you plan to establish and make a profit, then your goal is simply to make the most of the business you get.

But what if you aim to please all customers? Then, you would not only get that sale, but you would also get that customer to come back again and again.

Since we're talking about long-term goals and success, it makes sense to make sure your sales goal is to be the best at what you do to please your customer in such a way that he won't even consider going elsewhere for his needs.

In your business, you need to keep your marketing and sales techniques focused on creating and keeping your customers.

Sales for Success

Taking this step further, you also need to take into consideration your sales skills. As a successful entrepreneur, you need to carefully consider how you are selling, how effective you are, and how you can improve it in the short and long term.

If you can't sell, you can't succeed in your business. At close range, you're finished.

First, as a business owner, you must be able to sell yourself. Are you the business person that you are:

- Accessible
- Pleasant
- Friendly
- Educated
- Dedicated?

Or are you the guy everyone runs away from when they come to your door? Selling yourself as a trusted resource of information and products is the best way to become the man you trust.

In addition to this, you also need to

effectively sell your product to your customer. This also goes along with marketing your business for success.

In short, if you cannot sell your business successfully, then you have no business in the business. Learn to get excited about your own product. Then, learn how to successfully sell it to those around you.

You need to do this first before you encourage or train someone else to do it for you. Being enthusiastic, enthusiastic, positive and surely invigorating is the way to go in this case. If you don't feel comfortable talking about your product or business with your closest friends, how can you sell it to a complete stranger?

Here is the final result of marketing and sales. If you can't succeed in getting your product out there and getting others to see it the way you do, then you can't find success with it.

Sales experience is essential for sales to happen. Having sales; it means having customers who will come back to you. That means long-term success for you as a business owner.

ENTREPRENEUR SUCCESSFUL

Principles to remember and use

1. Start your business with a focus on your long-term success.

2. Establish and maintain goals that can be achieved with long-term objectives.

3. Manage growth carefully, without hindering your long-term profits.

4. Understand your market and how it belongs to it.

ENTREPRENEUR SUCCESSFUL

5. Be a trendsetter, with caution.

6. Learn from the good and bad of your past.

7. Invest wisely, decide wisely too.

8. Grow wisely without waste.

9. Manage your funds with prudence, rigor, frugality, and care.

10. Learn how to market your business correctly and effectively.

Final thoughts

In a world that focuses on the here and now, it is crucial for your own well-being to keep an eye on your future.

When, you use wise business practices like the ones we have discussed in this e-book; your goals end up being quite beneficial. Not only can you find success for your business today, but the long-term future of your business is more assured.

A business is an investment and can go in any direction (good and profitable or bad and expensive). When you start on the right foot, providing the right tools, the right

knowledge and some principles for the way you run your business, you find yourself more able to steer in the positive direction of your business.

It doesn't matter if your business is huge and worth billions of dollars or if it is an entirely new business. The goal is to give you the principles that can help you grow and prosper.

If you take the time to analyze, run, and then come back and start over each of these aspects in your business, the end result is success.

It's your money. You can spend it however you want. Using these key principles will help you have a successful business that adds dollars to your pocket over the years by maintaining a market presence.

Visit our author page on Amazon and get more MENTES LIBRES!

http://amazon.com/author/menteslibres

If you wish, you can leave a comment on this book by clicking on the following link so that we can continue to grow! Thank you very much for your purchase!

https://www.amazon.com/dp/B082K7N6LL

www.ingramcontent.com/pod-product-compliance
Lightning Source LLC
Chambersburg PA
CBHW070804220526
45466CB00002B/544